Fut Sao Wing Chun

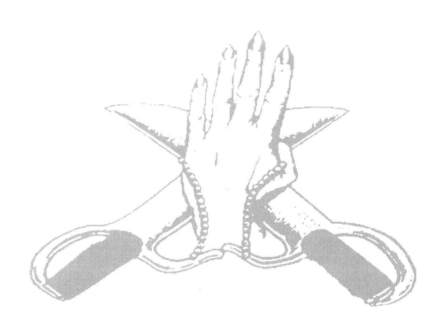

Fut Sao Wing Chun
The Leung Family Buddha Hand

By James Cama

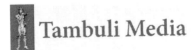

Tambuli Media

Spring House, PA
www.TambuliMedia.com

DISCLAIMER

The author and publisher of this book are NOT RESPONSIBLE in any manner whatsoever for any injury that may result from practicing the techniques and/or following the instructions given within. Since the physical activities described herein may be too strenuous in nature for some readers to engage in safely, it is essential that a physician be consulted prior to training.

First Published August 15, 2014 by Tambuli Media

ISBN-13: 978-0692222720

ISBN-10: 0692222723

Edited by Mark V. Wiley

Interior by Summer Bonne

Cover by Tyler Rea

Dedication

I dedicate this book to my sifu,
Grandmaster Henry Leung,
for all his teachings and wisdom.

I also wish to acknowledge my current sifu, Robert T. Lee. I am especially proud of my son, James Cama Jr., and daughter, Emily Cama. I would like to thank all my students and also my good friends, David Diaz and Angelo Quinto. Special thanks to Dr. Kenneth Fish, Arthur Glass and Dane Smith. To Travails Croom for his help editing the first draft. This book was made possible by my friend, Dr. Mark Wiley.

In appreciation of my mother, Emily Cama.

And in memory of my father, Joseph Cama.

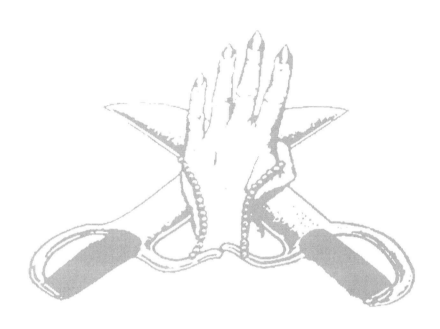

Contents

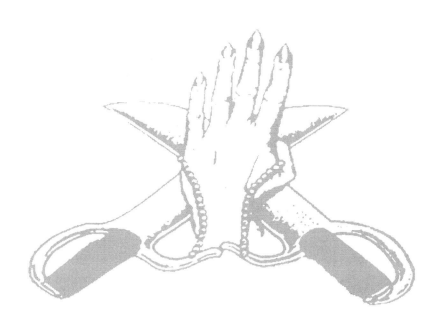

Foreword

I began my own study of Wing Chun in 1985, in various schools of Yip Man's version of the style. In the late Eighties and early Nineties, I read a few articles on other styles of Wing Chun that were older and had more material in their curriculum than the ever-popular Hong Kong version of the art. During this time I met Sifus Robert Chu, Rene Ritchie and Y. Wu and wrote forwards to and worked as editor on their joint book, *Complete Wing Chun*, and Rene's follow up, *Yuen Kay San Wing Chun*. I also edited Alan Lamb's three volume series, *Explosive Combat Wing Chun*. These books featured various styles of Wing Chun, some of which are not well known and are different than the popular styles. But, there seems to be little printed information on the Fut Sao (Buddha Hand) system from Mainland, China.

And so it gives me great pleasure to write this forward to Sifu James Cama's book, Fut Sao Wing Chun: The Laung Family Buddha Hand. It is a unique system and Sifu Cama is one of the top masters of the art. Like many people these days, we met on Facebook and developed a friendship. I enjoyed his postings of photos and video clips of him and his class demonstrating Fut Sao Wing Chun and Jook Lum Southern Mantis. Of course I had to reach out and see if he would publish a book with Tambuli Media.

The good news is that he said, yes. And just happened to be in the midst of a manuscript on this rare art. So he sent it to me and we worked together to develop the manuscript into the book you now hold in your hands. I know that this book will offer new insights and education within the Wing Chun community and will be a collector's item, as it is perhaps the only book in English on this rare line of the art.

I salute Sifu James Cama for this effort to promote and keep alive the art of his teacher, the late grandmaster Henry Leung. And for those less familiar with the Romanization style used in this book, they are reproduced in the way the last master Henry Leung preferred.

—Dr. Mark Wiley
Publisher, Tambuli Media
May 16, 2014

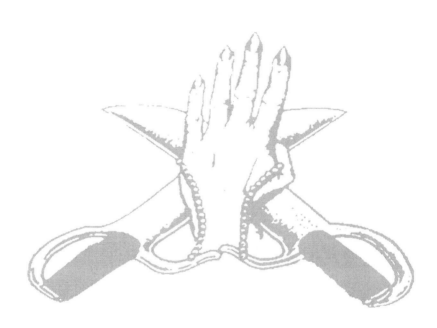

Foreword

I first met Master Henry Leung when he opened the Friendship Restaurant on Delancey Street in lower Manhattan. I had been introduced to him by an acquaintance who knew I was looking for a martial arts teacher. It was late afternoon on a warm spring day—Master Leung was behind the lunch counter serving a few customers. He looked up at us with a broad grin—slim, with a mischievous twinkle in his eye, he welcomed us and bade us sit at a table while he finished up.

Master Leung came over after the customers had left and my friend introduced us. Sifu Leung was straightforward and easygoing. He was very intelligent and well educated—he spoke English (quite well when the mood struck him), several dialects of Chinese, modern and court Japanese, and he could read German. In addition to a medical degree, he held a degree in economics from Tokyo University.

Henry Leung was born into a very well to do family in Foshan, China, and trained in his family's system of martial arts from a very young age. He was one of the most highly skilled yet unassuming martial artists I have ever met. We talked for a little while, then he told me to show up after school the following day and he would begin teaching me Fut Sao Wing Chun – also known as, "Buddha Hand Wing Chun."

I had little idea what I would be doing that day when I showed up for training. It was my first experience with Chinese martial arts, and I had only vaguely heard of the system Master Leung was teaching me. In those days Chinese martial arts were still very much kept within the Chinese community, and taught mostly behind closed doors. Master Leung led me down to the basement of the restaurant, which was set up like a gym—there were a couple of bags hanging from the joists, a wooden dummy, and numerous jars filled with dark herbal medicine. He taught me one movement at a time, first having me follow along with him, then perform the movement on my own, then leave me to practice until he returned. This same scenario was repeated almost daily for about two-and-a-half years. Sometimes the venue would be changed to his apartment across the street. During this time I only occasionally saw one or two other students; most did not stay very long as the training was hard, monotonous, and did not produce the instant results they were seeking.

One exception to this was James Cama. Master Leung mentioned him to me after James had been studying with him for a while. Sifu was impressed by how hard James worked, as well as with as his dedication. For his part James was also of great help to his Sifu—he stood by him through thick and thin. James and I met briefly at the restaurant one night, and it was obvious to me that he was putting everything he had into studying under Master Leung.

I lived abroad in Taiwan for the better part of the 1970s. Master Leung wrote letters of introduction for me to several martial arts teachers and organizations in Hong Kong. When I visited Hong Kong I sought out the contacts he provided. It very quickly became obvious that Master Leung was held in very high esteem among the martial arts teachers in Hong Kong and everyone seemed to know who he was.

When I returned to the U.S. in the early 1980s I continued my studies with Master Leung. It was then that I got to know Sifu Cama, and saw him more regularly. By then Master Leung had perhaps five or six students who had been with him for a number of years. In my opinion the only one who had received and absorbed in-depth training from Sifu was James—and it is also my opinion that he was the only one whose skills reflected our Master's teaching.

Sifu James Cama is the only one of Master Leung's student's to whom Master Leung gave written permission to carry on his teachings and to open a school. Since then, Sifu Cama has taught the Buddha Hand Wing Chun system to a limited number of students—carefully, with attention to detail, like a craftsman in his workshop.

Sifu Henry Leung left us late in 2011. We are fortunate that Sifu James Cama carries on the tradition of his teachings.

—Dr. Kenneth Fish
Pillow, Pennsylvania, 2009

Author's Preface

This book was written for the express purpose of sharing with the world the rare art of Fut Sao Wing Chun. This art, which was originally known as Gu Yee Chuan, or "Ancient Chivalrous Fist," is said to have been passed down through the Shaolin Temple's inner abbots. This art evolved into Fut Sao Wing Chun. Monk Goa Jhi Fut Sao taught my sifu, Henry Leung. Sifu was very pragmatic and evolved the system for use in modern times. He would test his skills against all arts and adjust himself and his art accordingly. I continue with this process and have expanded the system with the help of Sifu.

I wish to share this knowledge so that the art can flourish and grow. This book is special because for the first time ever Fut Sao's Advanced Siu Lin Tao form and its two man set are revealed. Every movement has a meaning and is examined. One should come away with a good look at the "inner gate" knowledge of this once "closed door" art. The gem of the art is its internal practices which are rarely seen in Wing Chun. As such, the hei gung (breath work) set and meditation/visualization practice is also shown here. This is a complete system.

While no book can capture the complete essence of a martial art, I have tried my best to offer enough material for the reader to gain a pretty good understanding of the Fut Sao Wing Chun system. I endeavored to show two of the three versions of the first form, Siu Lin Tao, of which most branches of Wing Chun have only one version. I also tried to discuss and show enough other training materials and techniques for one to see just how this Mainland, China branch of Wing Chun differs from the more popular Hong Kong versions.

This book is broken down into four sections and 10 chapters. An overview of the history and development of Fut Sao Wing Chun from China to New York City, is followed by a discussion of its many forms. After this is a pictorial demonstration of the Advanced Siu Lin Tao form and the Siu Lin Tao two-man form. From here we move into weapons, dummy and equipment training, followed by discussion on chi sao (rolling hands) and other sensitivity training and internal development methods.

I hope you enjoy this book on Fut Sao Buddha Hand Wing Chun, and that all interested parties reach out to me personally for information on learning the art. My contact information is in the back of the book.

PART 1

History And Tradition

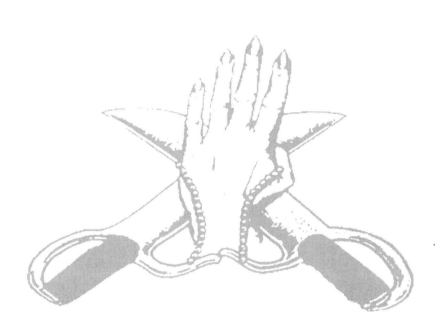

CHAPTER 1

Evolution of Fut Sao Wing Chun

[Note: The history and evolution of Fut Sao Wing Chun provided here was related to the author by Grandmaster Henry Leung.]

Wing Chun has flourished in the Fut San province of Canton, China. Laborers and merchants alike have taken to the art. The main attributes of Wing Chun boxing is its ability to be calm in motion and to conceal strength through suppleness. Wing Chun can be practiced in a space of a few feet or a small room. Fut Sao Wing Chun emphasizes short, close strikes such as poking and tearing. The ma bo (horse stance) is a narrow bent knee stance. Suppleness is key to overcoming brute force. Scholars and businessmen as well as common folk can learn this art.

Origins of Wing Chun

There are many versions of the origin of Wing Chun. These origin stories have been passed from generation to generation. Most did not know the details of the art's beginning. History has written that Tamo (Bodhidharma) created the 18 Arhat Boxing to strengthen the monks at the Shaolin Temple. Tamo revived the weak monks and restored their vitality. Their physical frames became fit and strong. The transmission of Tamo's method passed to monk Gok Yuen Sheng Yan who enhanced Tamo's teachings. Monk Gok Yuen Sheng Yan came from Yin Chou City and was known as Sung Yok. His secular name was Chiou. He beseeched Tamo to take him on as his disciple. Tamo taught him until his death, after which Gok Yuen Sheng Yan expanded the 18 Arahat movements to 72. He then traveled throughout the country and settled at Lahn Chou, where he met Lee Mok Lung and Bak Yuk Fung, whom he accepted as students. Lee Hok Lung adopted the monastic life. Lee Hok Lung learned both the skills of Bak Yuk Fung and the monk

Tamo (Bodhidharma)

Gok Yuen Sheng Yan. They combined their three methods to create a 108 movement system.

Lee Hok Lung created the six-and-a-half-point staff form called Lukh Dim Bun Kwan now famous in Wing Chun. The art was then passed on to Abbot Fa Hoi who then taught Ng Moi, Jhi Hsin, Bak Mei, Fung Dou Dak, and Lee Ba Hsan. Lee Ba Hsan died without passing on the art. Fung Dou Dak escaped the attack on Shaolin and studied Taoism at Mou Dong Mountain. There he learned the teachings of Jheong Sam Fong and became an important figure in the Mou Dong Sect. Jhi Hsin became Abbot to the Shaolin temple and Ng Moi lived in seclusion south of Ba Bak Hok Hong.

One day, Ng Moi observed a fox and crane in the midst of combat. The fox was defeated and this inspired her to create a natural system observing the sharp talons and facile movements of the crane. That was the creation of the White Crane system which influenced many other arts. She then traveled to Kwai Chou where she transmitted the art to Mui So En. They combined their knowledge and developed a new style, known as Fut Sao Buddha Hand boxing.

This was later passed down to Yim Yih Kung. Then to my Sifu's teacher, Kau Jhi Fut Sao (aka, Nine Finger Buddha Hand). Yim Yih Kung and Kau Jhi Fut Sao were the only ones to transmit the art of Fut Sao Kuen. When Yim Yih Kung's wife passed away he was left with his only daughter, Yim Wing Chun. He had no male heirs to pass on the art, as is customary; so he taught his daughter. After years of practice Yim Wing Chun became very proficient and after Yim Yih Kung passed away Yim Wing Chun taught her husband her father's art. When Yim Wing Chun died her husband Leung Bok Lau moved to Kwong Sai province to propagate the system. To honor his wife he named the style Wing Chun Kuen. Thereafter, the name Fut Sao Kuen ceased to exist in the secular world.

There are five styles of Wing Chun. Although they are from the same source there are differences between them. The five styles are: 1) Ku, the ancient style; 2) Juh, the village or red boat style; 3) Fat, the Buddhist original style, 4) Tao, the Taoist royal family style; and 5) Seong, the merchant style. The ancient style is lost today.

The Fut Sao Wing Chun Style

Fut Sao Wing Chun was brought to America in 1961 by Grandmaster Henry Leung, (Hong Lei, Chi Man), who trained and learned the whole system under the Great Master Gao Jhi Fut Sao. A great influence on Grandmaster Leung was the venerable Hsu Yun. He was the Dharma successor of all five Buddhist Ch'an sects of China, and he lived to be 120 years of age.

There have been several books written on the great Ch'an master Hsu Yun (1840-1959), two of which are pictorial biographies which were composed by one of his top disciples, the venerable master Hsuan Hua. The books tell stories about the life and times of the great master as he traveled extensively throughout China teaching and helping whomever he could. Also within the stories are descriptions of the tragedies and sufferings he endured as well as the victories and amazing esoteric powers that he acquired during his lifetime. One amazing story that took place in 1917, when the master was 78 years old. It relates how in the spring, eight workers were hired

The Venerable Hsuan Hua

to transport a huge Buddha statue from Kuan Yin Pavilion to Chicken Foot Mountain in Junggwo—a journey that would take quite a few days though treacherous mountain terrain, to places where no people had previously gone.

Ch'an Master Xu Yun (amitabhabuddha.wordpress.com)

One day while passing through Yen Jen mountain, the workers got the idea that there were gold and gems inside the Buddha, which influenced all the other workers not to carry the large Buddha any further. They all began saying that they had no strength left to do so. They raised their fee and would not listen to reason, complaining that they were being taken advantage of. The master Hsu Yun noticed a boulder nearby that was several pounds heavier than the Buddha statue. The master pointed to the enormous boulder and said, "Is this rock not heavier than the Buddha?" The workers quickly agreed that it was in fact two times heavier than the Buddha statue. The master then gripped the boulder with his two hands and raised it high over his head. The workers were in complete awe of this amazing feat of strength. They began to say this venerable master is a living Buddha and were more than happy to carry the statue through the mountain and were generously rewarded by the master upon reaching their destination. It is said: The Dharma protectors silently lent their aid.

In a small village in Canton, China the Leung family would have a boy born to the world two months premature. Henry (Chi Man) Leung survived, but being born premature created health problems for the young boy. The Leung family were devout Buddhists and were highly respected for their charitable deeds. Henry's father was a good friend of Gao Jhi Fut Sao and brought the boy to him in order to strengthen his health and spirit. Gao Jhi took

Grandmaster Henry Leung with Butterfly Swords

a liking to the young boy and taught him the Young Virgin Hei Gung light skills. As Henry grew stronger he was taught Gu Yee Chuan (Ancient Chivalrous Fist), the forerunner to Fut Sao (Buddha Hand) Wing Chun Kuen. Henry was younger and smaller than the rest of the other disciples. They constantly would abuse young Henry during sticky hands (Chi Sao) practice by pinching his chest. One day he came crying to Gao Jhi who comforted him and advised him, "Listen with your arms and absorb all

Grandmaster Leung and Sifu Cama play Chi Sao

their techniques." Before long, the victim became the victor. Within a year's time, young Henry had mastered all their hand techniques and made Gao Jhi proud and himself no longer a victim.

Henry Leung would be made a successor to the Gu Yee Chuan linage of Gao Jhi Fut Sao. In honor of his Sifu Gao Jhi Fut Sao, Grandmaster Leung renamed the style Fut Sao Buddha Hand Wing Chun Kuen.

Grandmaster Leung landed on the shores of New York City in 1961. Realizing he had in his possession a very rare and effective style of Wing Chun, and not forgetting his sifu's instructions not to teach the art of Fut Sao casually, he decided not to teach commercially. He instead began to hand pick his students, always teaching them behind closed doors. That is how I, James Cama, became his student and later became the first and only disciple certified to pass on the full transmission of the art. I have done so by hand-selecting specific students within my own kwoon.

The Tradition Continues

The arts of kung-fu are passed on to specific disciples through a ceremony known as the bai si. The Bai Si ceremony is one of the most honorable moments in a student/master relationship, as both pledge to each other and the previous masters of the lineage in front of the alter to dedicate themselves to each other and the art. The three bows and serving of the tea is carried out in specific ceremony. There is an exchange of Lacy envelope with lucky money from both student and Sifu. Once this is done the students have become family and are responsible for each other and the art.

Sifu Cama & James Cama, Jr.

Sifu Cama & Dane Smith

Sifu Cama & Peter Bonet

Sifu Cama & Mark Krivoi

Sifu Cama & Jack Mazolla

Sifu Cama & Tomas D'Amico

Sifu Cama & Elton Cohn

Sifu Cama & Bruce Nepon

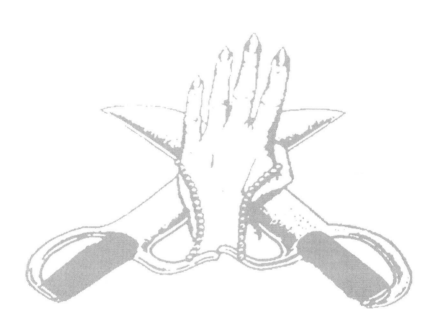

CHAPTER 2

Remembering Grandmaster Henry Leung

When I was a young man I was in search of this miraculous art of Wing Chun. By chance I met Master Moy Yat and became a "special student" and trained under him for about a year. His art was excellent but there was "something missing" for me. I was looking at an article by my good friend Bob Brown on a closed-door style of Wing Chun from Mainland, China called Fut Sao Buddha Hand. It told of this great master named Henry Leung. I called Bob and asked if I could meet Master Leung. He said that was impossible because Leung doesn't take in outside students. Bob said I could ask for Peter Chow and that he would train me in the art instead. He gave me the address to the Friendship Coffee Shop and I went the next evening! I walked into a crowded coffee shop and asked the middle aged man with a slight build standing behind the counter if Peter Chow were there. He looked me up and down and smiled. "Maybe he come later," he replied in broken English.

I waited for three hours as the crowd thinned. The man then tossed me a book titled, *Wing Tsun*, by Leung Ting. He said, "You want to learn this?" I shook my head yes, enthusiastically. He said to come back tomorrow morning. I arrived bright and early and the man approached me with a mop. Before I could utter a word he motioned for me to mop the floor. I started mopping, thinking to myself, What am I doing? A customer walked in and addressed the man.

Henry Leung Bong Sao and Kick

Grandmaster Leung and James Cama, 1978

"Hey, Henry, got a cup of coffee?" Henry nodded to me. With a smile on my face I served the customer. Thus began my relationship with Sifu.

My First Lesson

Later that day Sifu moved some tables and demonstrated the Siu Lin Tao form for me. He then told me to practice for one hour in ma bo horse stance. He then sat down, crossed his legs, and began reading the paper. Sifu sipped on his Hennesy and puffed on his cigarette. After 20 minutes I figured he wasn't paying attention so while holding the tan sao position I dropped the fist of my opposite hand down to rest. Without lifting his head, Sifu gestured for me to lift my fist back to chamber position. Then he turned the page of his paper and continued reading. From that moment on I never slacked off in my training.

The Test

One day, Sifu asked me about my martial arts experience. I told him I was a third degree black belt. He said, "Karate has good kick?" I said, yes. He said, "Kick me." I knew I had a very fast round kick so I thought I'd just place it next to his face. I said okay and threw it as fast as I could. The next thing I knew I was on the floor in pain, holding my groin. He counter kicked me to the groin! Sifu helped me up and said, "Karate has good grab punch?" Now I'm thinking, I have him now because the grab-punch was my favorite technique. He couldn't possibly get away. Sifu held out his wrist, daring me to grab it. I moved swiftly and could feel the hair on his wrist. The next thing I know, I'm again on the floor choking. Sifu helps me up and I bow deeply. "Please teach me, master."

The Incredible

One evening Sifu and I were in the basement of his building. I noticed that Sifu was exceptionally energized. I knew this because his color would change when he brought his chi (internal energy) up. He

James Cama, First Certificate Holder in Fut Sao

would turn a fading brown color and his lips would blacken. I also noticed his gait was nimble and quick. Sifu started to walk/punch vigorously toward an old piece of plywood shelving. His fist smashed the wood to bits, like an explosion. Then he grabbed a rattan pole and went over to an old metal door. Sifu whipped that pole and made inch-deep indents. Ten of them! I took the pole and swung it like Babe Ruth swung his bat. I barely made a scratch!

The Young Lion Challenges the Wolf

Sifu tells me that he has accepted the challenge of this young master of the Hung Kuen (Tiger/Crane) style. I begged Sifu to let me fight him for him, but he refuses. The young master came in and yelled, "I came to challenge your Fut Sao." Sifu motioned for him to attack with a calmness that was unsettling. The young master leapt with incredible speed and strength. His claws were ripping ferociously at Sifu. I was about to jump up when Sifu deftly trapped the young masters hands. Sifu then returned the claw and sent him flying across the room in semi-consciousness. I then threw him out and rushed back to Sifu. He smiled and told me that like Fut Sao he reflected back the young master's aggression without letting it touch him.

Meeting of the Grand Masters

One afternoon in New York's Chinatown Sifu was walking and noticed the gait of a slight man coming towards him. They immediately sensed each other's energy and smiled. They walked into a nearby coffee shop and sat down. The gentleman took his pipe out of his pocket and stuffed tobacco into it. He then rubbed the end with his forefinger and thumb. A flame rose as it lit. Sifu smiled. This is how Henry Leung met the great Lam Sang, the late grandmaster of the Kwang Sai Jook Lum Tang Lang Pai Southern Mantis Kung-fu system. I later had the great fortune of becoming a disciple of this rare art as well.

The Transmission

Years passed by and I became a closed-door disciple under Grandmaster Leung. Eventually I became the first student to finish the entire Fut Sao system and to be certified to teach the art of Buddha Hand Wing Chun. Sifu Leung taught the system secretly for so long and because training was difficult at times, many students never finished learning the whole system. In fear of the art becoming extinct, and with Grandmaster Leung's blessing, I decided to open the gate and teach the art publicly. Classes are held weekly at the Hong Ching Chinese Freemasons in New York Chinatown.

Grandmaster Leung and James Cama, 1994

PART 2

Hand and Weapon Forms

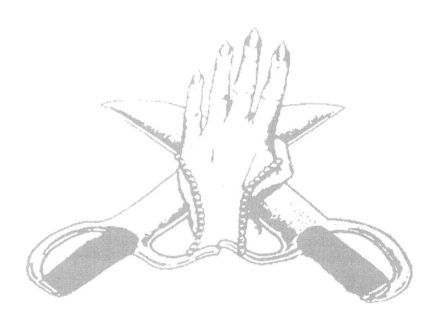

CHAPTER 3

Overview of Fut Sao Forms

It is important to realize that the opening to all of the forms in Fut Sao Wing Chun is a key to the methods and concepts of the entire system. The opening into the ma bo stance has hidden meanings. There are footwork patterns, kicks, knee checks, and knee strikes in the seemingly simple first opening steps. The footwork patterns are the beginnings of the siu baat gwa ("little octagon") movement. The kicks are front, diagonal, side, and sweeping. The knee checks and knee strikes are to the front, diagonal, and sides. The arm raise represents the outer gate application of the tan sao technique. The pull back is the jut sao technique and side body protection. So much in so little—that is the essence of Fut Sao Wing Chun.

Siu Lin Tao

Siu Lin Tao translates as "The Little Transmutation," and is also known as "The Beggar's Hand." As the fundamental mode of training in the Buddha Hand tradition, students dedicate at least four months of training this particular form and a test must be passed before one can advance to the next training level. Contained within this form is the synthesis of the entire Fut Sao Wing Chun system. It develops what is known as heavy nei gung (internal root power), horse stance, and an internal/external transmutation. It contains the essence of all three of the basic forms, Siu Lin Tao, Cham Kiu and Biu Gee. And even though the form is performed in a stationary standing posture, hidden with its "non-movement" are footwork and kicking techniques. We'll look more deeply into the second and third Siu Lin Tao sets in the next chapter.

Cham Kiu

Cham Kiu translates as "Depressing Bridge," and is also known as "Riding the Horse." This is the second mode of training in the Buddha Hand tradition, student must dedicate four months to training the form, and passing a test, before they can move on to the next training level. This form utilizes full body movement within the four torque directions, utilizing vertical, horizontal, and angular left and right directional movement. Cham Kiu develops monkey footwork, angling, locking, grappling, snake body, crane hand, fox direction, and light skills for moi fa pole training.

The Cham Kiu form is the basis for the fighting concepts of the system. It is the first form which shows a unique siu baat gwa footwork used for angular attacks, and teaches many angular attacking combinations. Moreover, Cham Kiu develops how to bridge and lock up an opponent. It also emphasizes the low horse (up and drop down movements). One learns how to move the internal organs to enhance chi circulation and ging (kinetic) power. It introduces the chi body sensitivity and teaches bridging, joint dislocation and manipulation.

Biu Gee

Biu Gee translates as "Thrusting Fingers" or "Darting Fingers," and is also known as "Poison Snake Hand." This advanced form develops internal ging (emitting power), vertical, horizontal and angular torque, yin and yang energy (e.g., expulsion/absorption, flying/eating chi), loose hands, fa ging (explosive force), finger strikes, inch shock, and scary powers. One can touch an opponent's pressure points and strike with an internal burst of energy. A minimum of four months is spent on this form before moving on to the next level.

Fut Sao Biu Gee also contains grappling, chin na (seizing, locking), low horse fighting techniques, and anti-grappling techniques. Organ movement and breath retention is emphasized in this form. It shows one low horse kicking and punching technique and compact, subtle strikes are done with explosive power (ging) and chi body for subtle evasiveness. Elbows are executed in pointing and penetrating strikes. Ten different kicks are shown in the form, which also develops high level internal chi body sensitivity and evasiveness. Vibratory inch power generation is trained within the movements of the form. Biu Gee emphasizes finger techniques using full body power, to attack pressure points and nerve cavities (dim mak), which are structurally weak so the opponent cannot respond as effectively, giving the practitioner a formidable advantage.

Siu Baat Gwa

Siu Baat Gwa translates as "Little Octagon," and is the eight-directional movement and footwork set. As the fourth mode of training it teaches one how to use vertical, horizontal, and angular bisecting movement, utilizing full body movement to enhance ging power. Movements are made with chi body sensitivity for full body evasiveness and striking. The form contains biu gee finger striking and chi palm techniques. The four powers of float, swallow, sink, and spit are also trained in this form. Siu Baat  Gwa is a "change and invisibility" set containing angling, circling, spinning, stealth, and circle walking movements and techniques. One month minimum is spent on the practice of this form before moving on to the next.

This evasive, invisibility set puts one in an advantageous position for an immediate counter strike. This is a very rare form that is exclusive to Fut Sao Wing Chun. In fact, it incorporates techniques from all the previous levels of training, and combines them with advanced footwork, allowing the student to quickly place themselves in a position where their opponent is weakest. It is a close boxing system which emphasizes accuracy, balance, speed, roundness, flatness, and slightness.

Two Man Forms

Two-man forms are prearranged attack and counter attack exchanges between training partners that emphasizing techniques taught in each form. There are two-man forms for Siu Lin Tao, Cham Kiu and Biu Gee. These forms help the practitioners develop a sense of distance, fighting spirit, body conditioning and release of the fear of confrontation.

Lukh Dim Bun Kwan

Lukh Dim Bun Kwan is the Six and One Half Point Staff form. It is taught either with a six or eight foot staff and is a highly complex and tactical set that teaches long range fighting and pointing. Training with the long pole helps to develop thrusting power in chi sao (sticking hands) practice. This form takes at least six month to perfect.

Baat Jam Do

Batt Jaam Do are the "Eight Slash Butterfly Knives," also known as "Pig Skinning Knives." The form develops incredibly fast slicing techniques, which teach cutting power and short ging for use in chi sao and loose techniques. This form also takes six months to perfect.

Esoteric Vagabond Weapons

Fut Sao Wing Chun also makes use of what are known as the six esoteric, vagabond weapons. These include: bladed fan, double dagger flute, flying meteor balls, turtle darts, iron monkey ring, and chop sticks. It teaches you that anything can be a weapon.

Mok Yahn Jong

The Mok Yahn Jong or "Wooden Man Dummy" form is known as the "Fut Sao 108." In addition to training the form on the wooden man dummy, this form is also performed on a stake post, a sliding dummy in a low horse stance, and with weapons. This advanced form is the culmination of the Fut Sao training curriculum, and includes the major concepts of all previous forms in addition to advanced fighting and dim mak techniques.

Nei Kung & Hei Kung

The nei gung (internal work) and hei kung (breath work) sets in Fut Sao Wing Chun are very rare Shaolin forms that hail from a small village in Canton. They are necessary internal training sets for the development of the heavy horse, light skills, ging, inch power and dim mak. These sets are rarely taught in Wing chun but have been well-preserved within the Fut Sao system.

CHAPTER 4

A Study of Siu Lin Tao

The Siu Lin Tao form may be the first taught in Fut Sao Wing Chun but it is the most important. The postures reflect fetal positions. From creation to birth is when we are internally our strongest. Fetal postures are reflected in hand positions known as tan sao, fook sao, fut sao and many more. Sui Lin Tao develops many concepts. The center line and its cutting angles are the main concepts. Defining inner/outer gates is another. The body's boundary areas is yet another.

Every movement in the form has meaning. Siu Lin Tao combines the theory of yin/yang, internal/external. It's performed in a flowing, smooth manner even though it does have fast, powerful movements.

There is also hidden footwork, knees, and kicks within the form in addition to chi palm and clawing techniques. There are also ways of transmuting of the mind, body, and spirit and techniques for developing chi transference by moving internal energy throughout the body. The form especially teaches how to perfect spinal erection in order to maintain root and chi flow for power.

Hei Gung, or "internal breath work," is done throughout the form with specific control. While many Wing Chun systems breathe in and out with each movement, Fut Sao includes a specific breath-holding sequence within the form. Here's how to do it:

1. **Breathe in for a count of 4**
2. **Hold your breath for a count of 16.**
3. **Breathe out for a count of 8**
4. **Hold for a count of 4**

Siu Lin Tao teaches the practitioner the "Four Principles" and the "Eight Actions." The descriptions of these that follow are those of my Fut Sao Wing Chun classmate, Dr. Kenneth Fish.

Fut Sao's Four Principles

The 4 principles of tun, tu, fou, and chen describe both movements and the qualities of movements. They may describe specific hand techniques, but also outward, grossly visible body movements as well as movements within the body.

1. **Tun** literal means "to swallow" and describes the hand motion of lightly contacting and redirecting downward and outward while following the incoming movement of a strike. In terms of body movement, it describes compressing the body (visible) and contracting the body inwards (not visible).

2. **Tu** literally means "to spit" and describes expelling or reversing the force of the above movement, tun; like a spring expanding outwards. As a hand movement it is the response to the deflected strike. The two movements together are like a ball being compressed and released, or a rubber band being stretched and then released towards a target. The body motion is a vertical release of the compression and contraction.

3. **Fu** literally means "to float" and describes the quality of movement when touching the opponent's arm or body—light and insubstantial. It also describes the quality of the body and footwork—light, insubstantial, uncommitted, able to follow, and "float" with the opponent.

4. **Chen** means "to sink" or "to be heavy" and describes the quality that the opponent feels when you touch him or execute a movement— heavy, downward pulling, being forced into place. It is also an arm movement—the sinking bridges that are the opening to the set of the same name. It also describes the vertical contraction of the body onto the arms, which transmit the force to the opponent.

Fut Sao's Eight Actions

The so-called eight peerless actions describe hand and foot movements and also have body movements (both visible and subtle or internal) associated with them. The first two actions are described in more detail, while the last six are just defined here. If you'd like to know more about these "secrets," feel free to reach out to me personally for instruction.

1. Bian means "to whip" and describes a quick flicking movement of the forearm, wrist, and hand. It also describes a wavelike motion through the entire body to power a seemingly soft strike.

2. Qie means "to cut through" and describes piercing through an opponent's defence. It is also a way of using force in a strike that feels to the opponent as if my palm or arm is cutting into him.

3. Wan means "to seize," "to pull against," and "to detain."

4. Zhuang means "to crash into," or "to bump against."

5. Tan means "to rebound" or "to spring" off of something.

6. Suo means "to contract," and "to withdraw" and also "to lock up" and "to entrap."

7. Pan means "to coil up," "to wrap up," and "to twist."

8. Chong means "to shoot out" and "to thrust out."

Fut Sao's Three Trained Forces

1. Jie jin is "joint force," wherein force is produced by the mechanical action of the muscles, tendons, and joints.

2. Zhi jin is "straight force," wherein force is augmented by the unified movement (external and internal) of the body.

3. Sheng jin in "rising force," wherein force is produce by the entire structure from the ground up. Every movement includes external and internal movements coordinated and moving in harmony.

These concepts are very complex and take years of training to comprehend and develop their subtleties. In the next two chapters I present to you the Advanced Siu Lin Tao and the Siu Lin Tao Two-Man sets of Fut Sao Wing Chun. While practicing those sets try your best to see how the information in this chapter is associated with them.

CHAPTER 5

Advanced Siu Lin Tao Form

Siu Lin Tao is the transmutation of the mind, body, and spirit. The form develops the internal chi and maps out the "inner-"and "outer gates" of combat as well as teaching to identify and protect the "center line."

Practice of Advanced Siu Lin Tao develops chi palm and the girdle energy and how to manipulate it. This builds energy in the fingers and palms to be used to strike points or grasp and claw, with seizing techniques known as chin-na. The form sequence develops fa-ging power in techniques and refinement of fist, finger, palm, and claw techniques.

Secret leg techniques are shown from knee checks to kicks. The front, diagonal, and side kick can be practiced in slow and fast motion over a chair. By holding on to the back of a chair you can rise up on your toes to develop the toe kick.

Note: In following these pictures of the form, repeat the biu gee (thrusting fingers: up/down, side/side) three times each, as shown on pages 38-39 and 43-45.

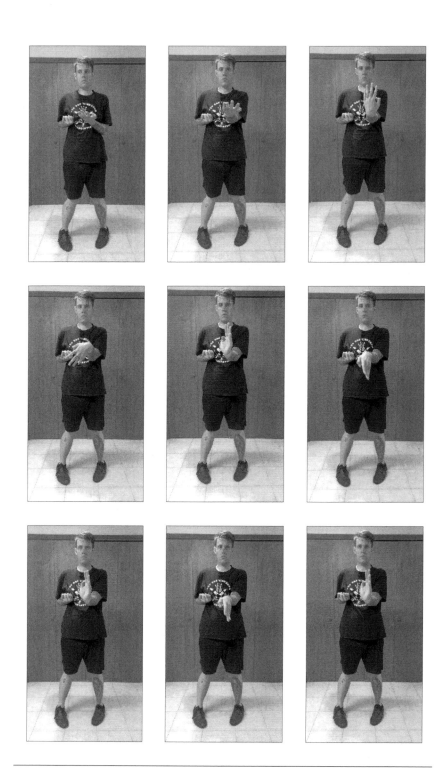

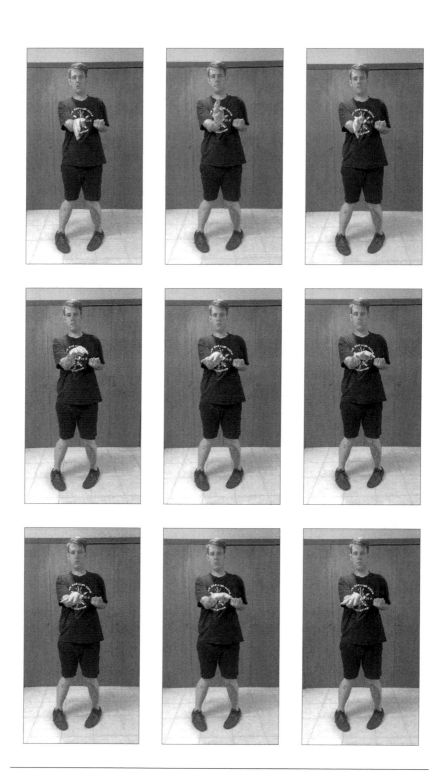

Side View

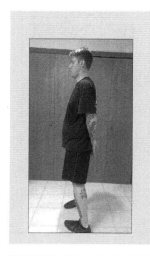  

CHAPTER 6

Siu Lin Tao Two Man Form

The Siu Lin Tao two-man set is a realistic way of practicing the applications of Siu Lin Tao. It teaches you at least one technique for attack and counter attack. It also teaches the correct point strikes and reaction speed. Once mastered one can move with speed and power in a realistic fighting mode.

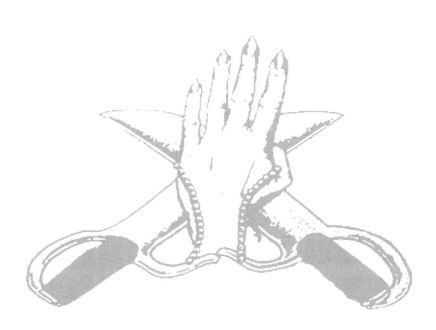

PART 3

Training Methods

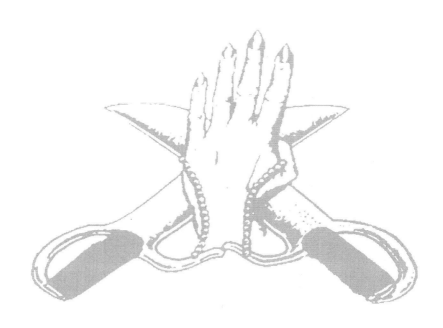

CHAPTER 7

Fut Sao Sensitivity Training

The Fut Sao Wing Chun system is both a hard and a soft style. Its softness allows a practitioner to overcome an opponent who is much larger or stronger by using sensitivity and technique. Sensitivity training is the way to develop an understanding and perception of the opponent's energy and movements. It's like having a sixth sense. It develops reaction in a "sensing hand" that can counter an opponent's techniques instantaneously. This has given Fut Sao Wing Chun an advantage over other styles because of the instantaneous aliveness of its sensing hand.

There are many methods, exercises, and drills within the Fut Sao Wing Chun that develop the type of sensitivity that allows you to sense, follow and redirect an opponent. A few of them are discussed below.

Don Chi Sao

Don chi sao is a single arm sensitivity training drill. This develops an individual understanding of sensitivity for each arm. Don chi sao works to develop sensitivity in each arm individually. This leads to two armed Chi Sao.

One starts by touching wrists in tan sao position. Then the inside hand palms the chest and the outside hand uses fook sao to block. The fook sao hand then punches and the palm hand blocks with a bong sao. The partners then return to the original tan sao position and repeat.

Lop Sao

Lop sao is a bridging and grappling exchange of hands which leads to many combinations of counter measures. Lop sao practice enhances speed in sensitivity. Once mastered one can quickly change-up the opponent and unbalance him.

Chi Sao

Chi sao is the famous Wing Chun sensitivity exercise that literally means the sensing of chi (energy) and how to control it. Once the sensing of energy is mastered then one can redirect the slightest of force issued by an opponent. Fut Sao chi sao is unique in that it helps develop and use sensitivity with not only the arm but the whole body—known as "chi body" in Fut Sao. This training and application skill is barely perceptible to the naked eye. The exercise is even done blindfolded to enhance the feeling of touch over sight.

Fut Sao also uses an "energy bridge" which creates in the opponent a false feeling, an incorrect perception of a movement. The opponent cannot sense your hand because he is feeling the energy and not your physical self. This gives one a forward pressure which enters your opponent before he can react. Fut Sao chi sao trains to apply the sinking, swallowing, floating, and spiting powers discussed in an earlier chapter. "Spring power" off of your opponent's energy or "coiling power" is also developed and used in chi sao practice.

Chi Sao Example Two

Chi Sao Example Four

Chi Sao Example Six

Moi Fa Chi Sao

Moi fa chi sao practice is carried out by standing on poles in order to work your balance and "light skills."

Chi Gerk

Chi gerk trains the ability to utilize the legs with sensitivity, like the arms. It teaches one how to counter kicks with leg checks and counter kicks. In this practice one learns to apply the hand positions of tan sao, bong sao, fook sao, and rolling with the legs and feet. True chi gerk experts are rare and this skill is one of the highest levels in Fut Sao Wing Chun.

CHAPTER 8

Fut Sao Training Devices

Part of what makes Fut Sao Wing Chun practitioners so effective is their use of training enhancement devices that help develop the internal and external qualities of the student. In addition to Wing Chun's famous wooden man dummy, Fut Sao also makes use of the following training devices. Let's look at the various training devices below.

Mok Yahn Jong

The Mok Yahn Jong "wooden man dummy" is used to develop proper technique and ging power. Dummy techniques are external strikes done with internal power. Many misunderstand the purpose of the dummy and strike it hard, like a makiwara post or punching bag. They pad the dummy and hit it as hard as they can. This is incorrect. The dummy techniques are internal and soft. Total body movement and ging power are used to strike it.

We have many versions of the mok yahn jong. In fact, there are five sets of forms played on the dummy: 1) Standing, 2) Low Horse, 3) Stake Siu Baat Gwa, 4) Baat Jam Do, 5) Lukh Dim Bun Kwan.

The Stake Dummy

The stake dummy is used in conjunction with the Siu Baat Gwa footwork and strikes (chi palm), wherein one circles the dummy and strikes all around it. The conventional dummy is used to develop ging power from the kickback after it's struck. The Bat Jam dummy is used to develop the inner cutting knife techniques. The pole dummy teaches the inner pole techniques. Low horse dummy develops lower body striking and kicking.

Chi Palm

The chi palm develops emission of internal energy into techniques by hitting a hanging sheet of paper. Hit the paper until it tears cleanly in the middle with one strike of the fingers. Chi palm is also developed by extinguishing a candle from a distance of a few feet chi emitted from a with a palm strike.

Iron and Translucent Ball

Holding an iron ball develops weight resistant training for internal and external strength. Iron ball training enhances and transmits chi through the hands and into the body. It also develops the bridge and forward energy. The translucent ball does the same as the iron ball but also enhances the practitioner's spiritual psychic abilities.

Finger Claw

The finger claw exercise develops strength and endurance in the hands, fingers and grip by contracting fingers into a fist; by squeezing a wax or clay ball; and by crumpling newspaper in your hand.

Chi Body Hitting (Iron Jacket)

In this training the "devise" is a thin stick or set of loose wound iron sticks. It develops the chi body (or "iron jacket") to be able to withstand an opponent's blows, by mastering internal breath while striking the body lightly with a special stick.

Chi Palm

The chi palm develops emission of internal energy into techniques by hitting a hanging sheet of paper. Hit the paper until it tears cleanly in the middle with one strike of the fingers. Chi palm is also developed by extinguishing a candle from a distance of a few feet chi emitted from a with a palm strike.

Iron/Bamboo Monkey Ring

The use of iron and bamboo rings helps to isolate techniques in a confined space to develop energy force (ging). This training helps one concentrate on their own boundary areas (gates) while having external resistance from the rings. It develops resistance strength and a flexible bridge by the arms being inserted into the rings and pressing out against the sides and rolling with them into various arm positions, like those used in chi sao.

Bridge Bar

The bridge bar develops resistance training and arm endurance by extending the arms out and holding up a heavy wood or iron bar for several minutes at a time. The bar can be 10 pounds and up to 100 pounds or more.

Pole Jut Sao Training

This series of moves develops the transference of energy through the pole shaft to its tip. The pole is held at shoulder height and with the hands at a shoulder's width. Strike down with jut sao repeatedly until the ends of the pole vibrate. The concept is to transfer energy from your body, through your arms and hands out through the pole. In addition to jut sao pulling techniques and fa ging energy strikes, this exercise also develops the low horse and long range energy strikes.

Bamboo Sticks

Fut Sao practitioners develops tough bones by rolling your hands and forearms over and under bamboo poles. You can use one or many sticks on top and bottom of the arms by rolling them back and forth on a table.

Iron Palm

Fut Sao practitioners develop the deadly iron palm by thrusting their hands into a bucket of mug beans. First, soak your hands with dit da jow (strike wine liniment); second, soak them in a container of one part white vinegar and two parts water with rusty nails; third, finish with an application of dit da

---

jow. After a while move from mung beans to striking hanging and stationary bags.

Sand and Water Jar

This develops grip strength and hand claws by gripping the opening of a jar filled with sand or water and doing the fook sao exercises.

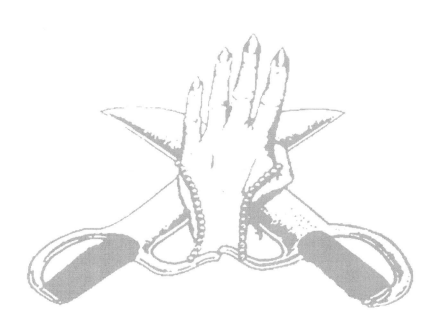

CHAPTER 9

Fut Sao Meditation and Hei Gung

Meditation is paramount in the development of chi and hei gung. Once one can visualize chi (internal energy in their body) then they will be able to circulate and transfer it through the body. The micro-cosmic are the energy centers in the internal body (also known as chakras). In training, the student first learns where these energy centers are located. They begin at the dan tien—located three inches below the naval—then move up to the solar plexus, heart, neck and top of the head. Remembering this sequence will be helpful in learning and practicing the following exercises.

Visualization of Chi

Concentrate on visualizing the micro-cosmic internal energy by imagining an energy sphere of white light. Sit comfortably with your palms held up. Stretch your spine and keep your chin tucked in. Keep your mouth closed and put your tongue on the roof of your mouth. Breathe in through your nose then breathe out through your mouth

upon completion of a full inhalation. Visualize your light sphere in your dan tian (field of energy) three inches below your naval. Visualize the energy rising up the front of your body to the crown of your head. Then bring it down your spine to your groin. Bring it back to your dan tian. Then raise it up to your chest. Visualize it going across your shoulders and down the outside of your arms. Feel the energy in your fingertips and palms. Then raise it up the inside of your arms to your chest. Lower the energy to the dan tian. Feel the energy rise up in the middle of your body until it is under your heart. Lower the energy down the outside of your legs all the way to your feet and feel the energy in the soles of your feet. Now raise the energy up the inside of your legs back to the dan tian.

Chi Transference

Like the above exercise, again visualize the white energy sphere in your dan tian. Move it in your mind down your left leg to your left foot. Feel the tingling and heat in your foot for a few seconds. Then bring the energy back up to your dan tian. Now do the same for the right leg. Concentrate on the sphere of energy in your chest. Visualize the sphere going down your left arm to the hand. Feel the tingling and heat for a few seconds and bring it back to your chest. Do the same for the right arm. Visualize the sphere in your third eye (the space on your forehead between the eyebrows). Move the energy down the front of your body to your groin. Move it back up your spine around the crown of your head. End by storing in your third eye.

Hei Gung Set

PART 4

Fut Sao in Action

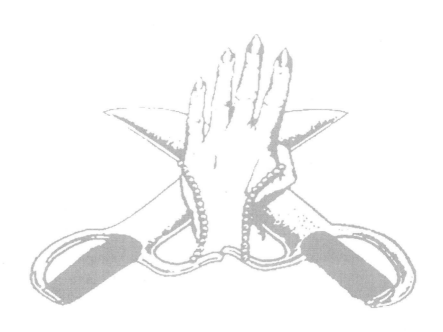

CHAPTER 10

Fut Sao Theory and Applications

Fut Sao techniques are done "live" (in real time) with total body connection. The internal power comes from the torque, internal breath and vibration of techniques. Absorb and reflect back an attack. Strike until you see red. Sense the openings with your arms and body. Strike completely and swiftly. Know your opponents strengths and weaknesses. In addition to these essential pieces of advice, as the kuen kit or saying of the art that follow.

Lo Kwai Kuen Kuit and Yiu Jee

1. As the opponent comes, you receive him.

2. If he goes, you escort him.

3. If contact is lost, you move forward.

4. Use soft to overcome hard.

5. Hard and soft combine when needed.

6. Use stillness to overcome movement.

7. Footwork is to be quick and nimble.

8. Body angle must be changed quickly.

9. Hands and feet defend as needed.

10. Attack the center, control the center, and destroy the center. Refers to attacking the centerline but also attacking the center of gravity of the opponent by joining to and controlling his center of gravity.

Mastering Stillness

Grandmaster Leung always told me that what is most important in an encounter is the opponent's energy and how to control it. The way to do that is to understand stillness. When meeting an opponent's bridge one counters with the exact force put upon him. Then one can be very still and wait for movement of energy and counter accordingly. Real softness is mastering the emptiness and filling the void.

Coiling and Spring Energy

Grandmaster Leung would tell me that your power comes from your body movement. To do this, envision a giant coil deep inside your body. When striking you contract it and then expand it explosively. Your counters should be springy and borrow from the opponent's energy. Everything depends on torque power. Torque comes from the toes up to the top of your head. Understand how to get power from the smallest of circles. This works in harmony with vibratory power. These are the seeds for inch, shock and scary powers.

Fut Sao Striking Hands

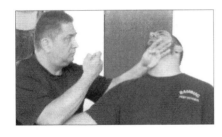 

Multiple Attackers Applications

Pole Applications

Knives Applications

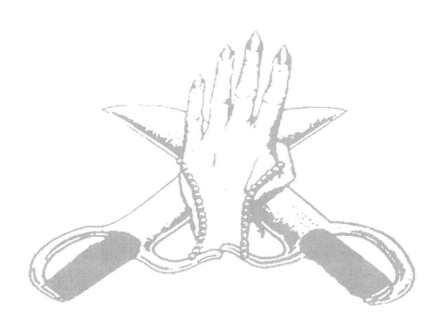

Conclusion

Fut Sao Wing Chun is an ever-evolving martial system which encompasses all the laws of nature. My sifu, the late Grandmaster Henry Leung, always said he wished he had named the system "Natural Style." He felt that all technique should be a natural reaction to stimulus. Sifu Leung would react like a clairvoyant and immediately counter anything that was thrown at him. It was eerie, yet incredible. Whenever I react to an attack, I let my arms move on their own. My training is part of my subconscious and comes out under stress. My Sifu would actually become calmer under fire. He truly had the "mind of no mind." His belief in his art was complete and unwavering. The opponent is ultimately important. That's where the focus must be. Sifu would watch an opponent's movement and immediately know his weaknesses.

To become like him one must first develop the body internally and externally. Practicing the curriculum every day is essential. Study the forms and their breakdowns. Master chi sao and fighting. Develop the floating, sinking, swallowing and spitting energy concepts. Remember to always fight from a place of righteousness and not to be abusive. Sifu believed in karma. He always said that whatever negativity you give out you will get back in return. He reflected back any aggression and negativity so that it would never internalize in him. Develop your mind, body and spirit and it will help you throughout your life. It saved my life.

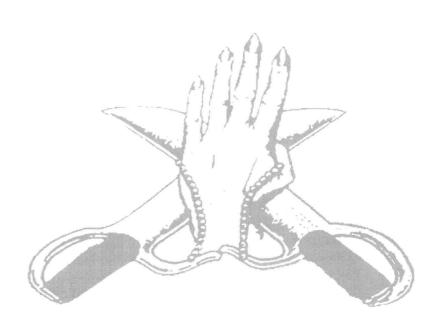

About the Author

James Cama began his martial arts training in karate at the age of seven under his cousin, and at age nine he trained formally at Sun Duk Son's Mu Duk Tang Soo Do dojang. He then trained in Hung Gar Kuen under Bucksam Kong and Chester Chin, Ying Jow Pai under Leung Shum, Goju-ryu Karatedo under Peter Urban, Kayo Ong and Meitatsu Yagi, Wing Chun under Moy Yat and Fut Sao Buddha Hand Wing Chun under Grandmaster Henry Leung.

Years passed by and Cama became a closed door disciple under Grandmaster Leung and eventually became the first student to finish the whole Fut Sao Wing Chun system and to become certified to teach the art. Sifu Leung taught the system secretly for so long and because training was difficult at times, many students never finished the whole system. In fear of the art becoming extinct and with Sifu Leung's blessing, Sifu Cama has decided to open the gate and teach the art publicly. This book, Fut Sao Buddha Hand Wing Chun, is one way he is spreading the art to the world.

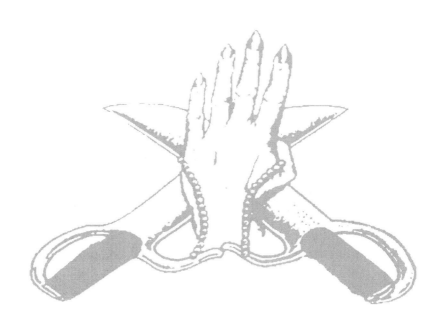

Tambuli Media

Excellence in Mind-Body Health & Martial Arts Publishing

Welcome to Tambuli Media, publisher of quality books on mind-body martial arts and wellness presented in their cultural context.

Our Vision is to see quality books once again playing an integral role in the lives of people who pursue a journey of personal development, through the documentation and transmission of traditional knowledge of mind-body cultures.

Our Mission is to partner with the highest caliber subject-matter experts to bring you the highest quality books on important topics of health and martial arts that are in-depth, well-written, clearly illustrated and comprehensive.

Tambuli is the name of a native instrument in the Philippines fashioned from the horn of a carabao. The tambuli was blown and its sound signaled to villagers that a meeting with village elders was to be in session, or to announce the news of the day. It is hoped that Tambuli Media publications will "bring people together and disseminate the knowledge" to many.

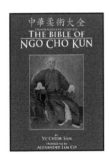  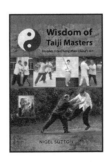 

www.TambuliMedia.com

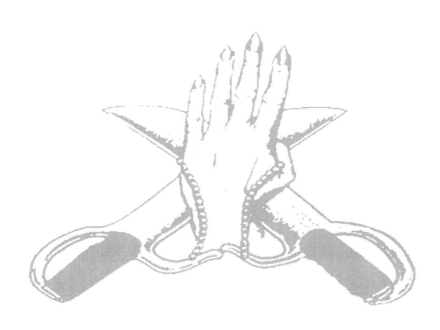